If lost Please

return to

_____

_____

This book is dedicated

to your smile

:)

May you believe in Magic,

Again!

——And

May that live within your

heartbeat everyday.

ε

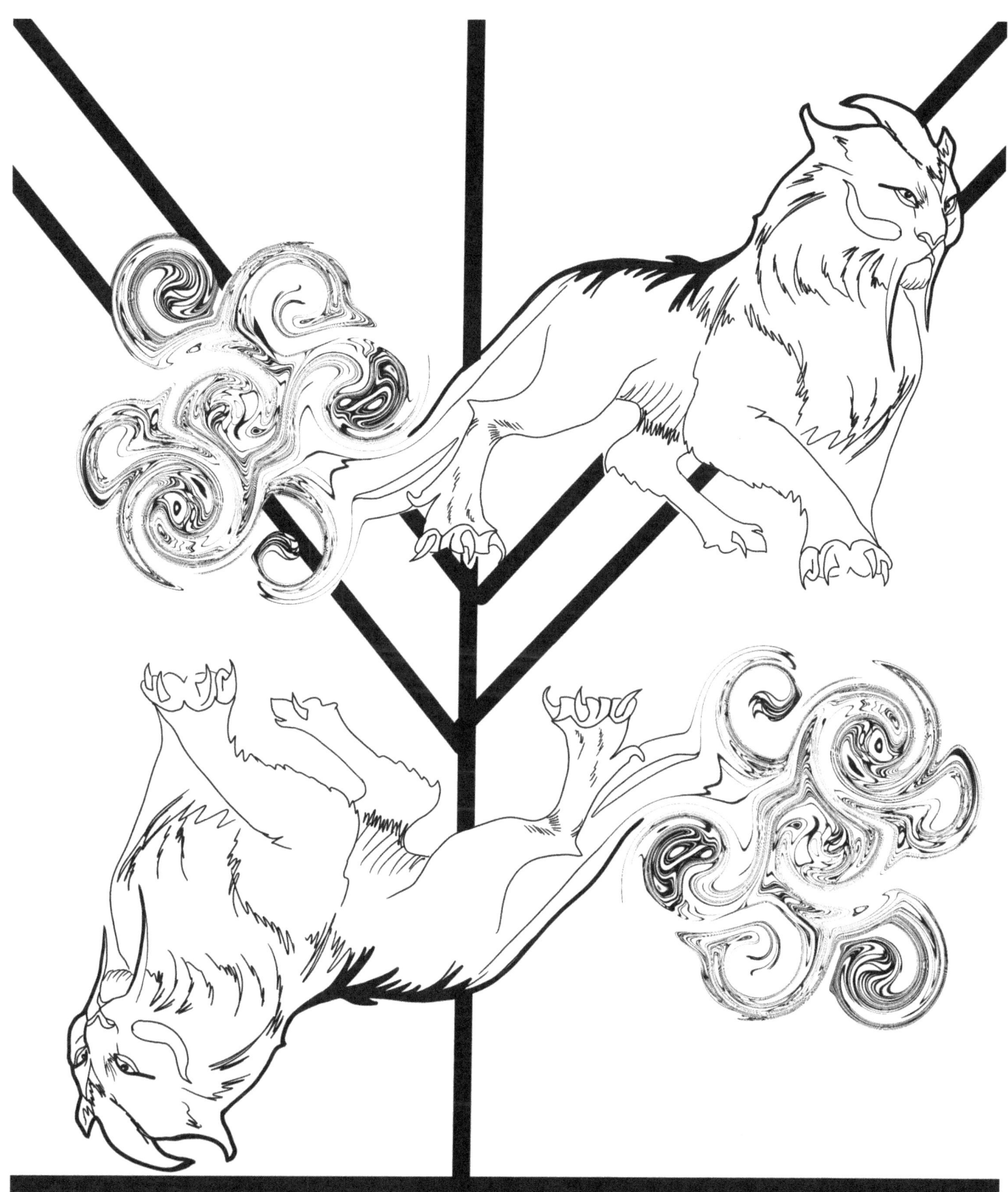

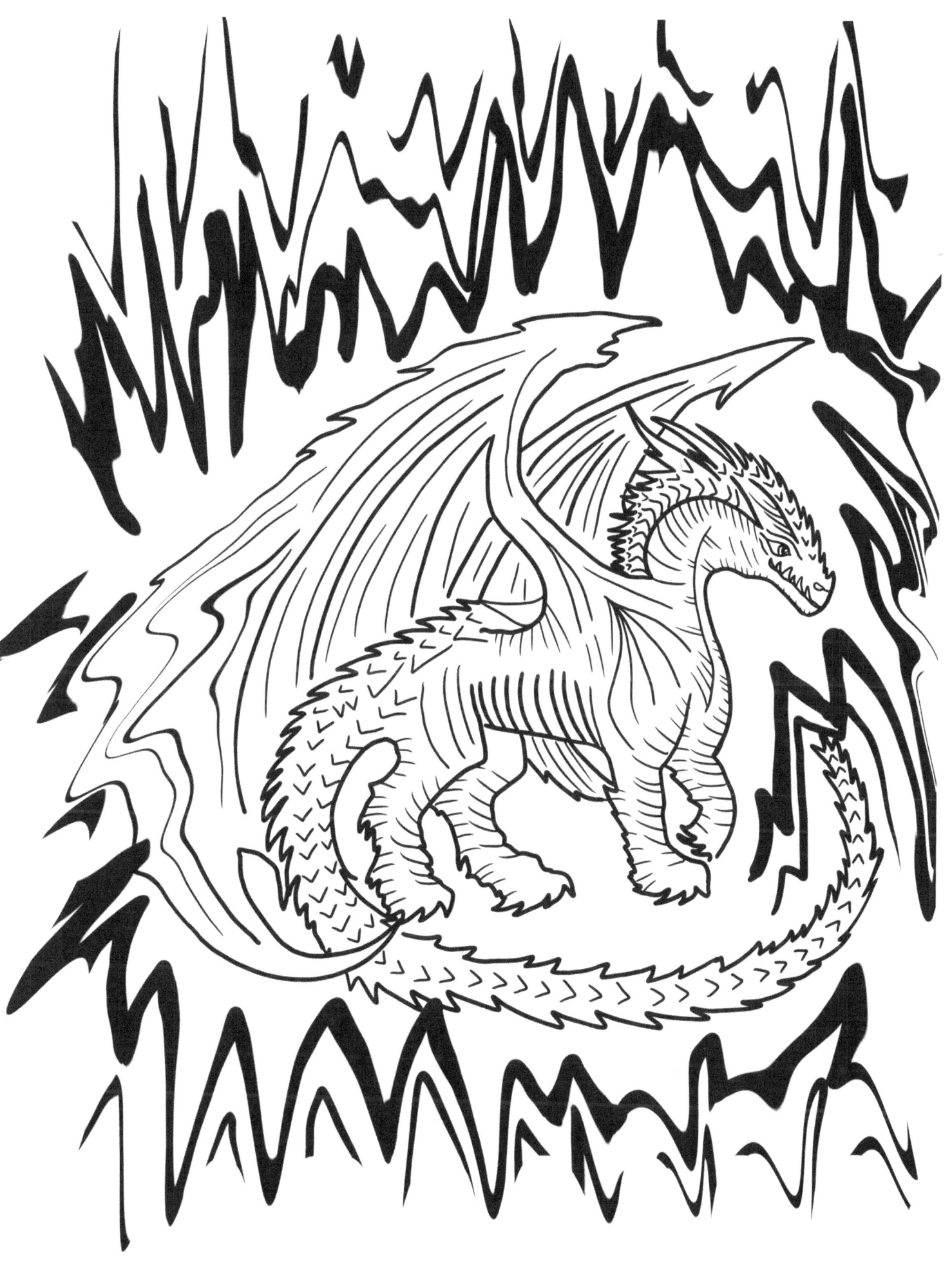

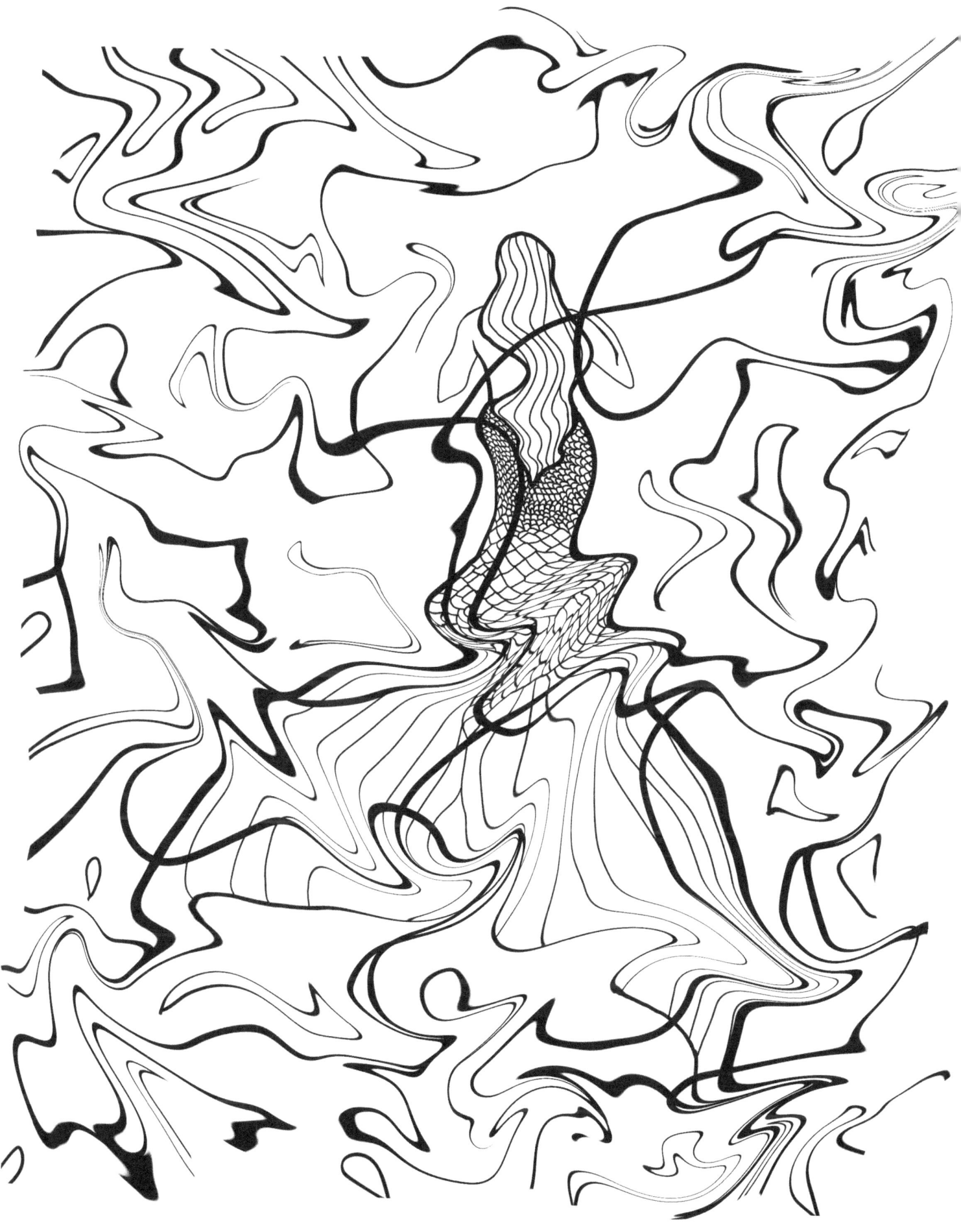

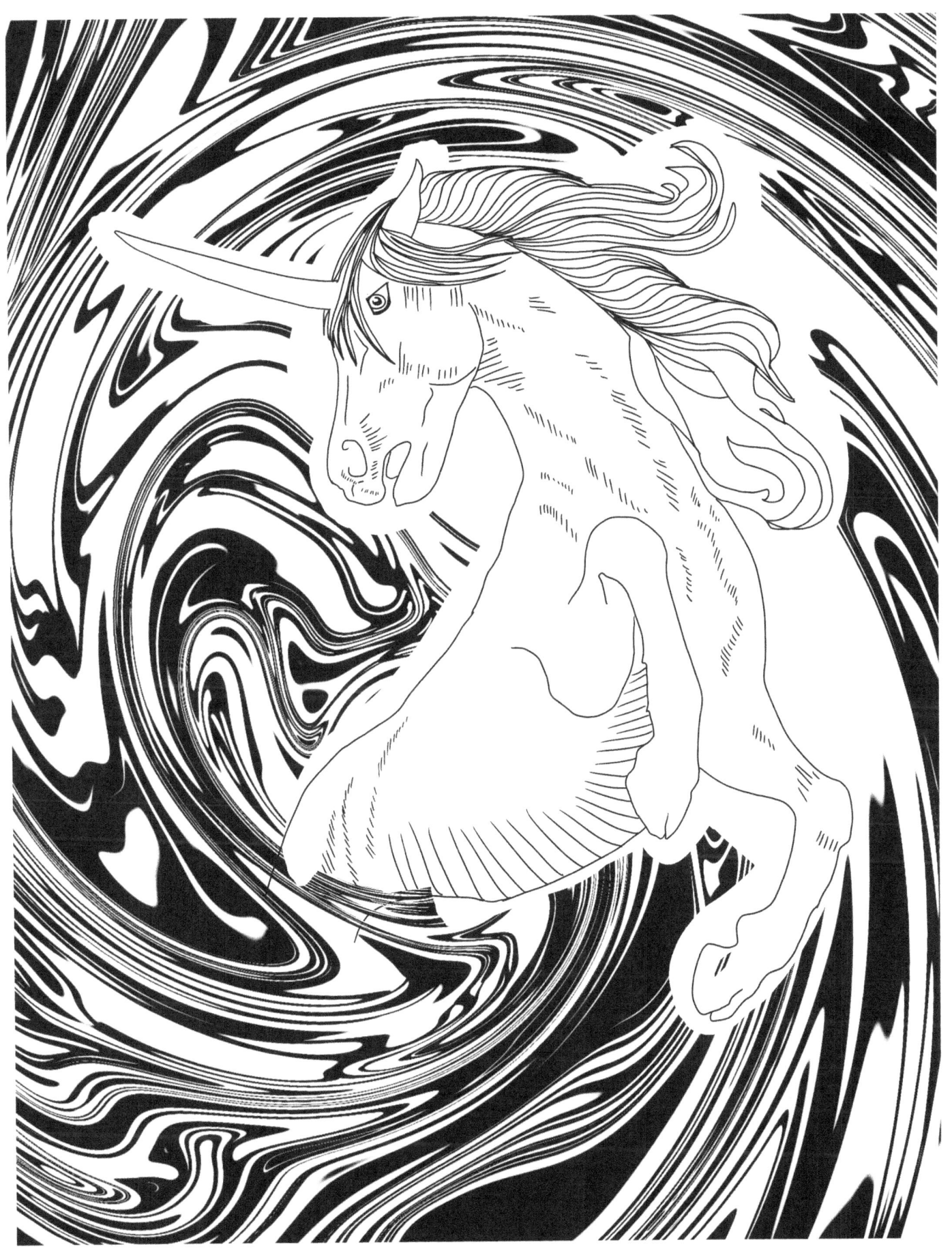

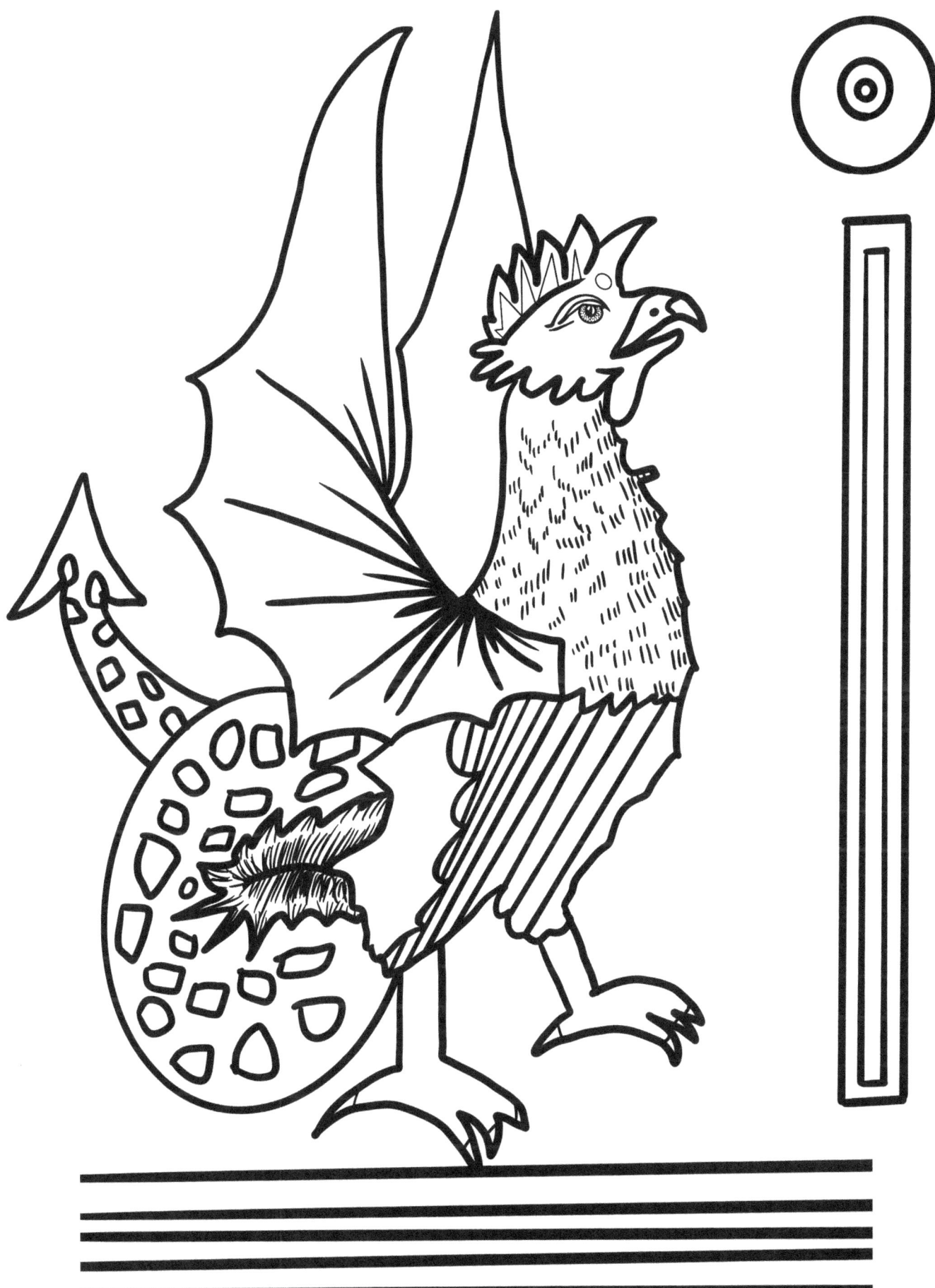

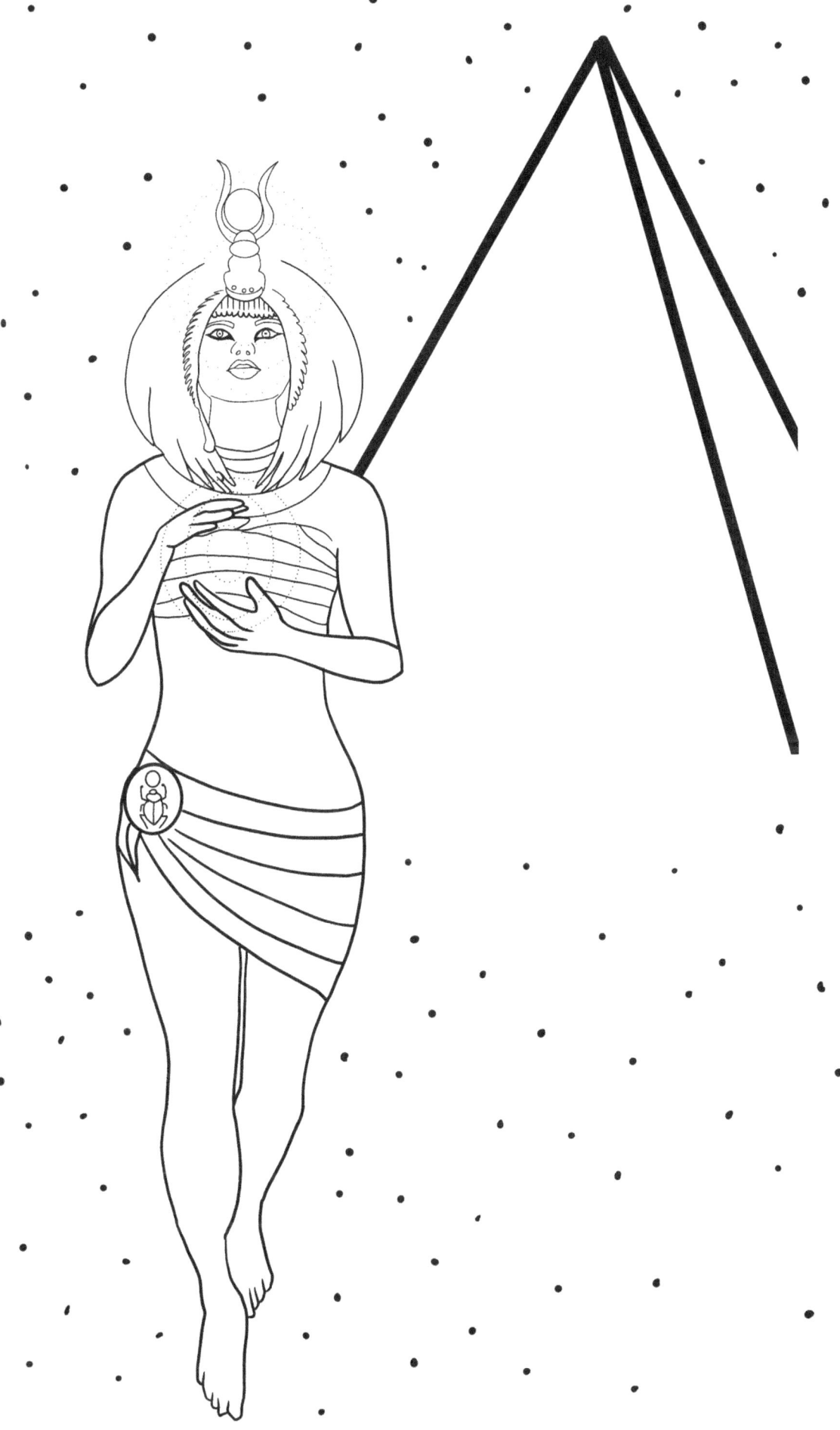

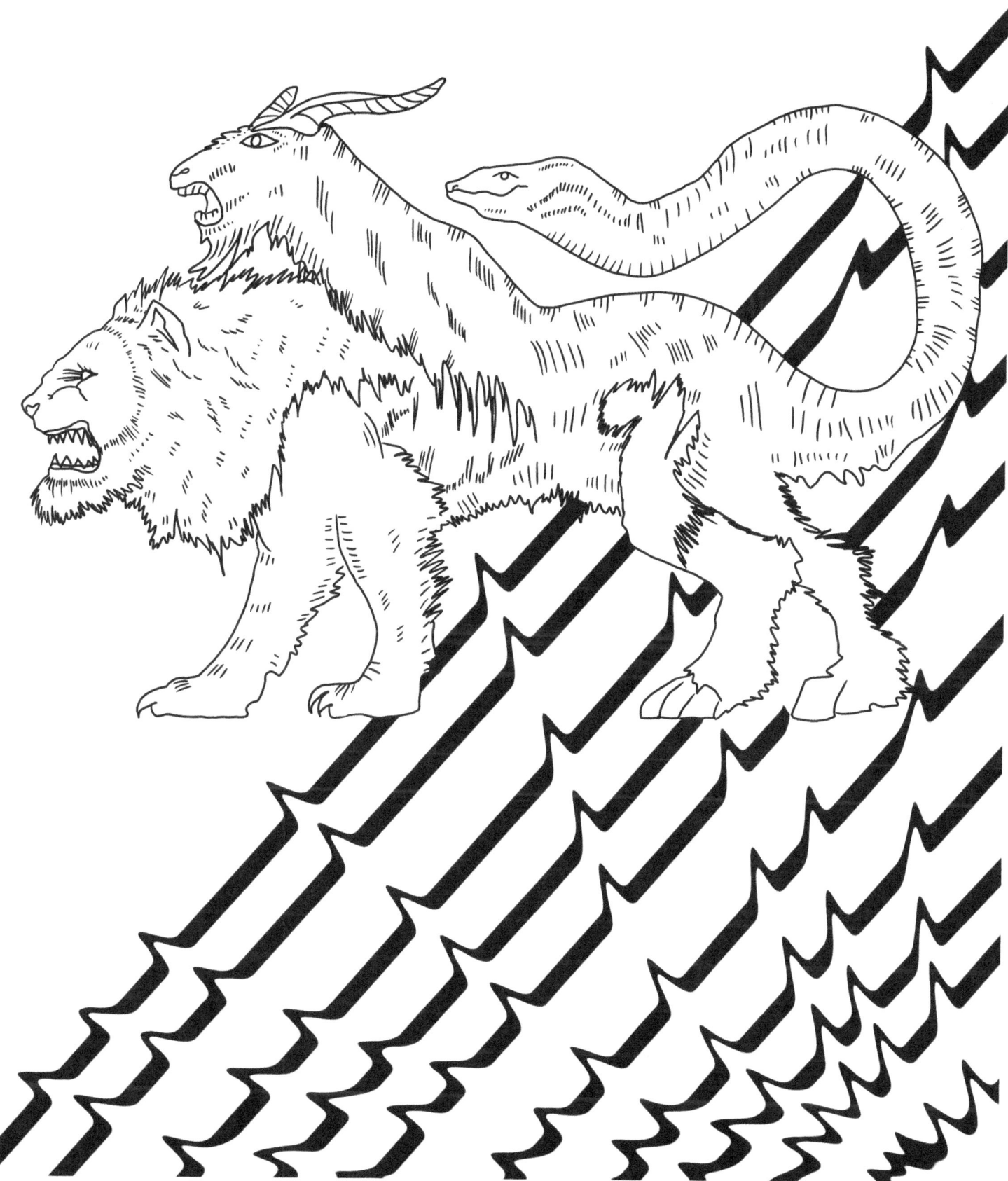

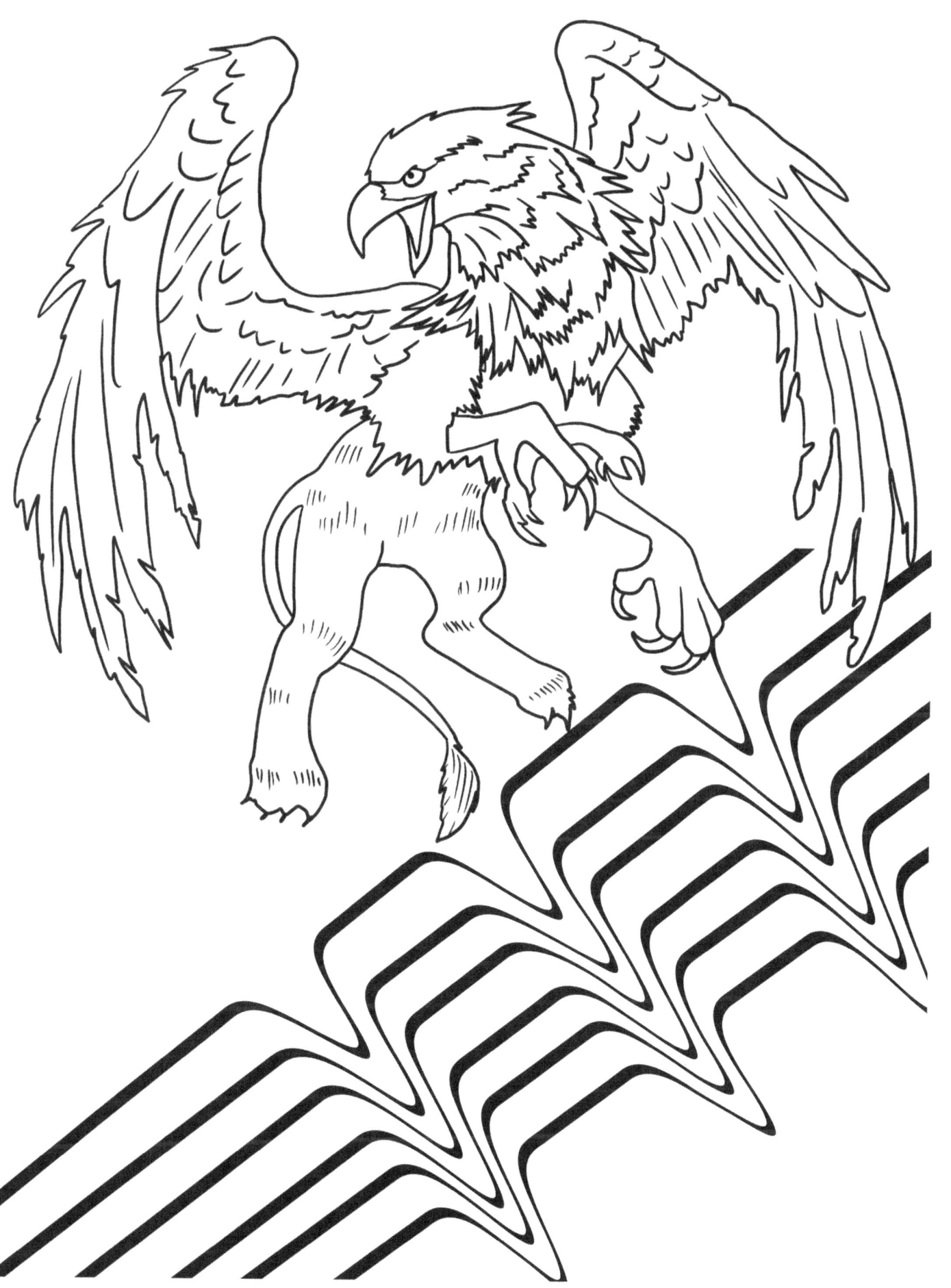

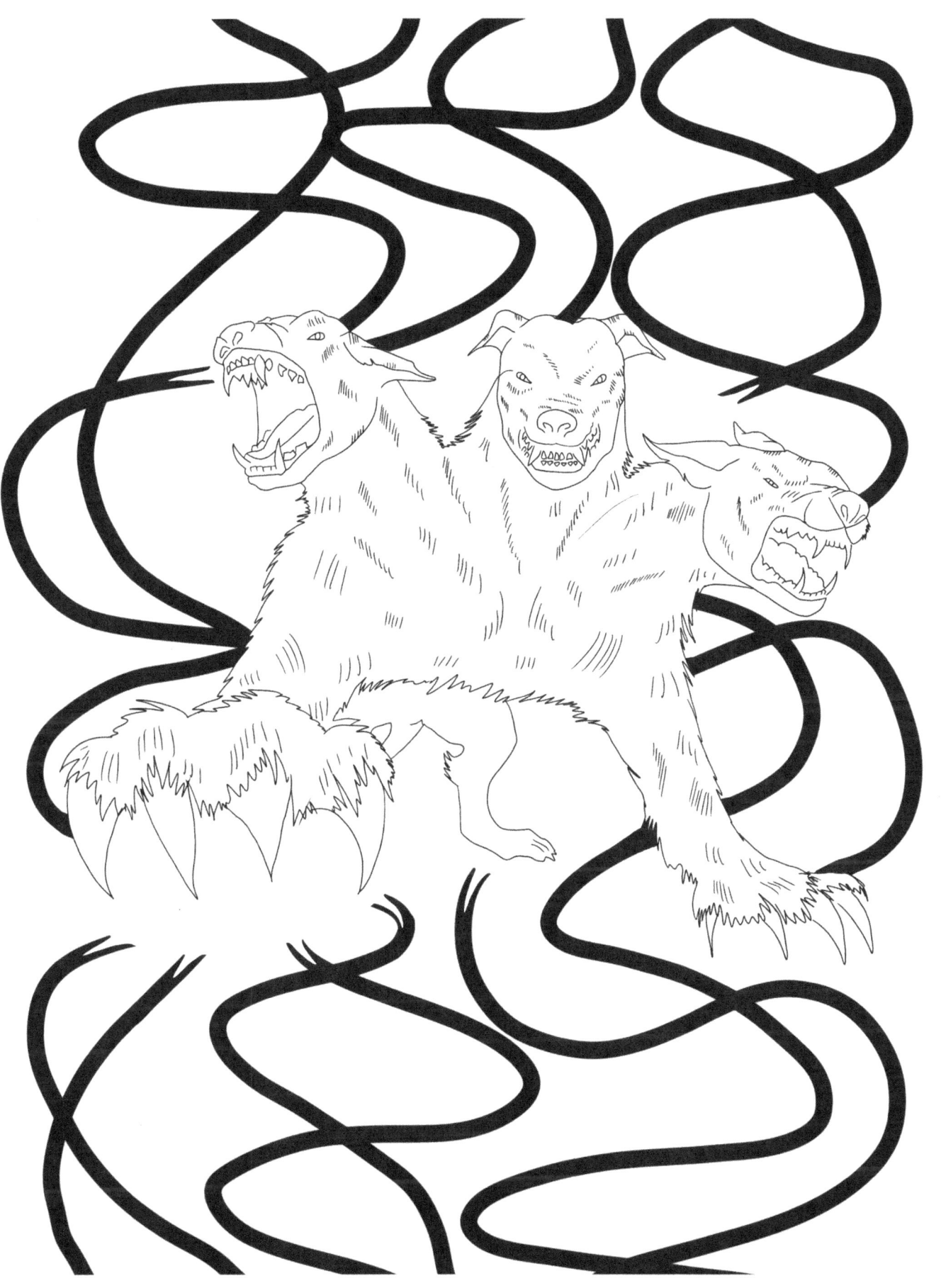

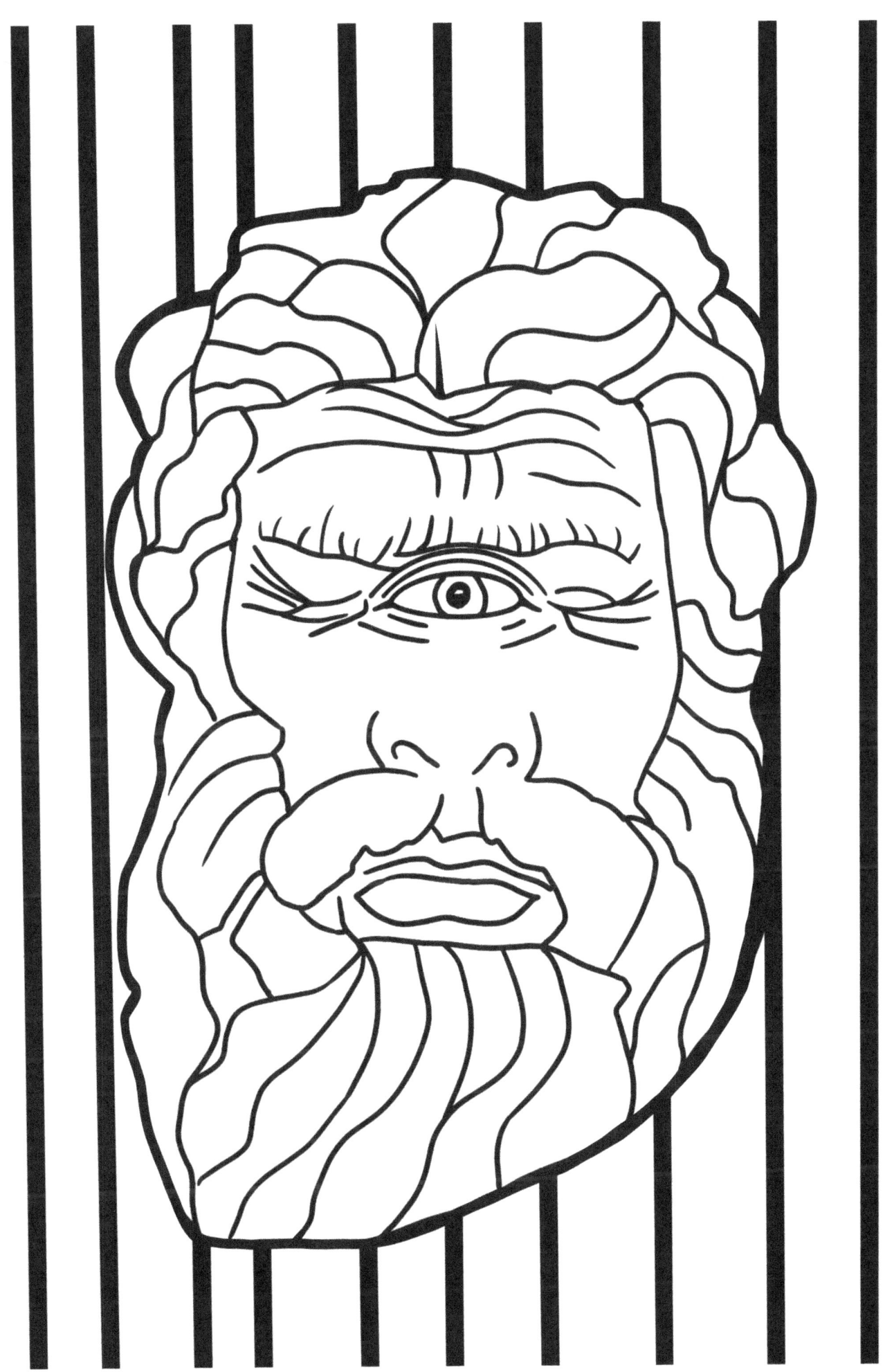

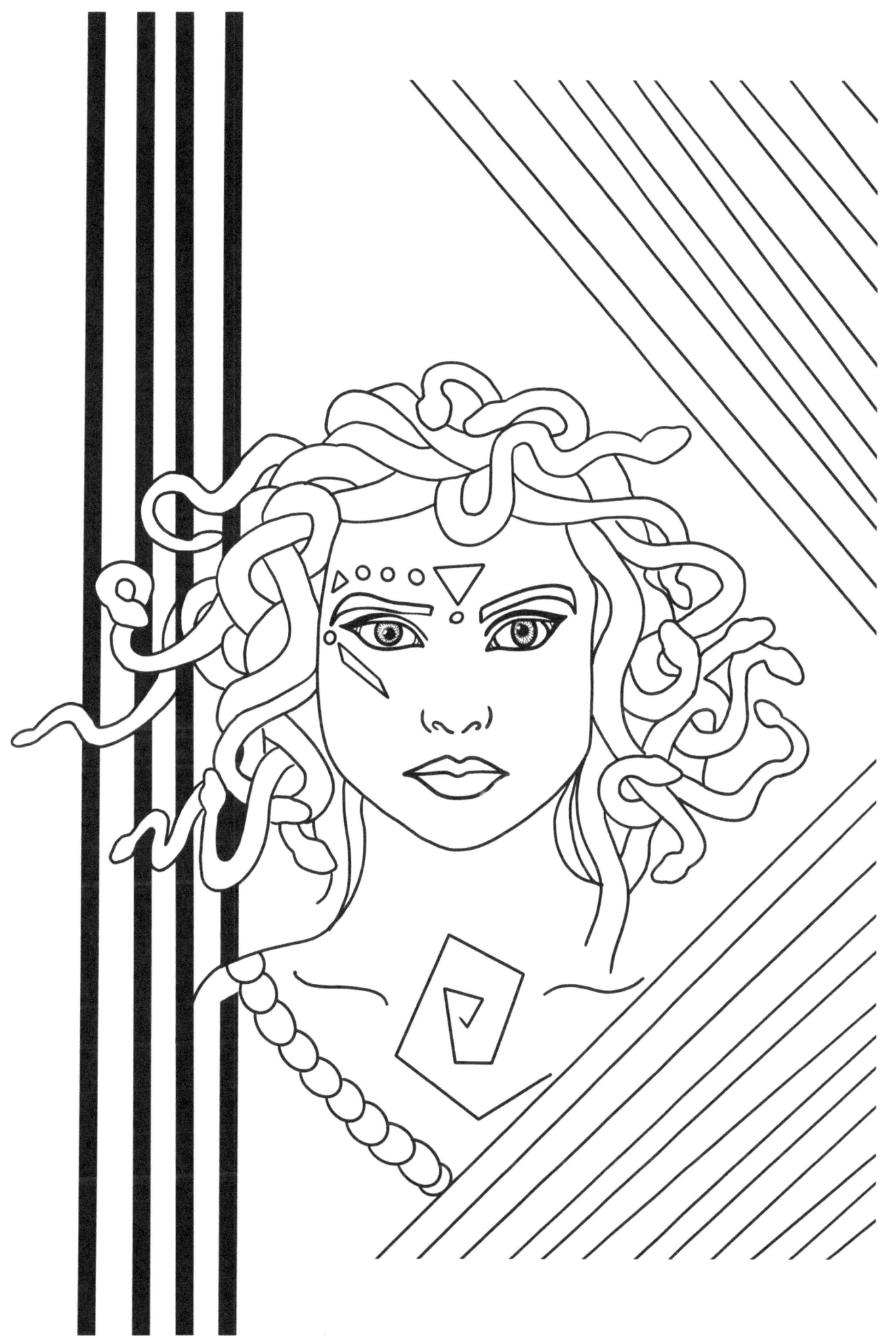

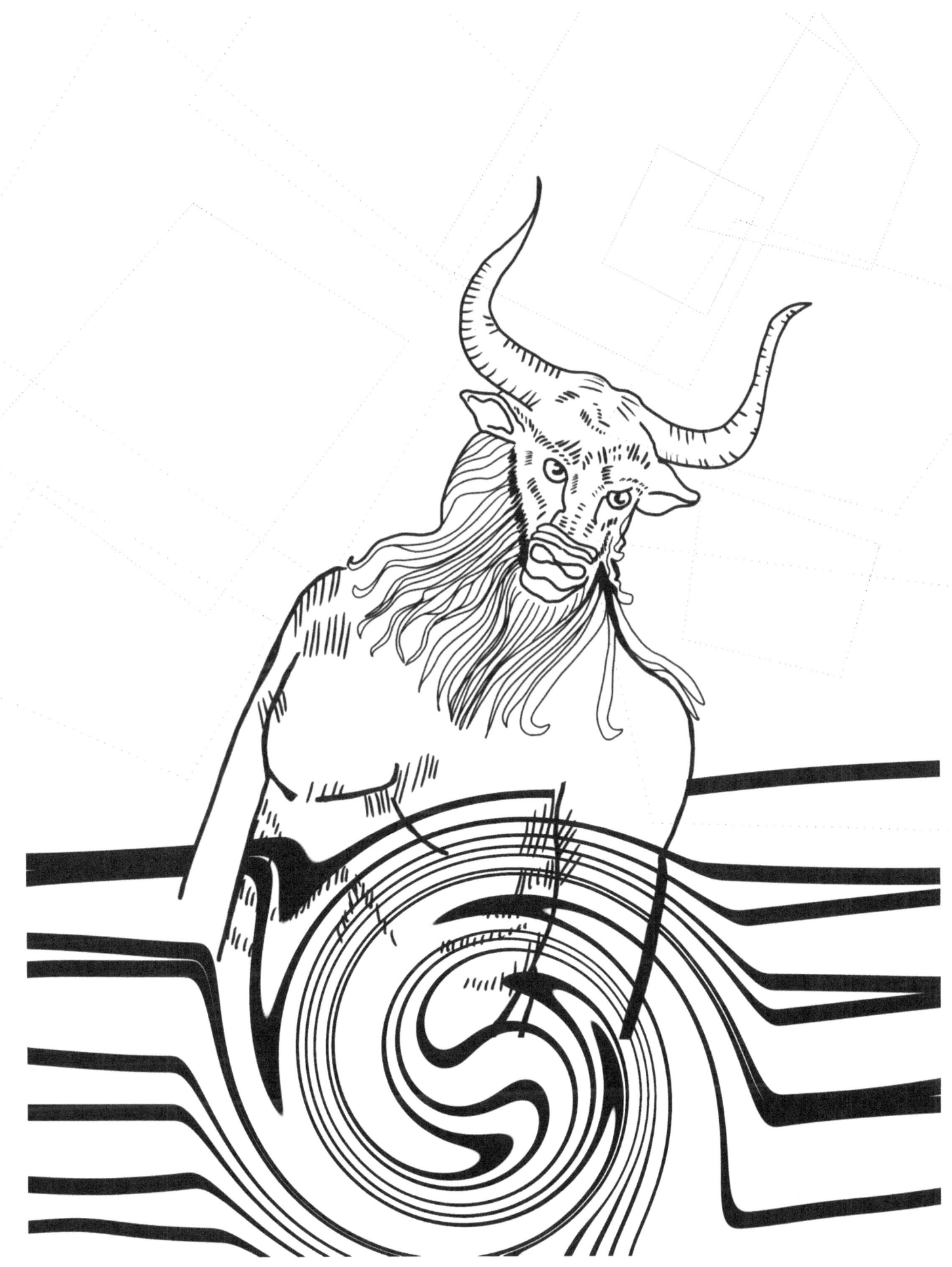

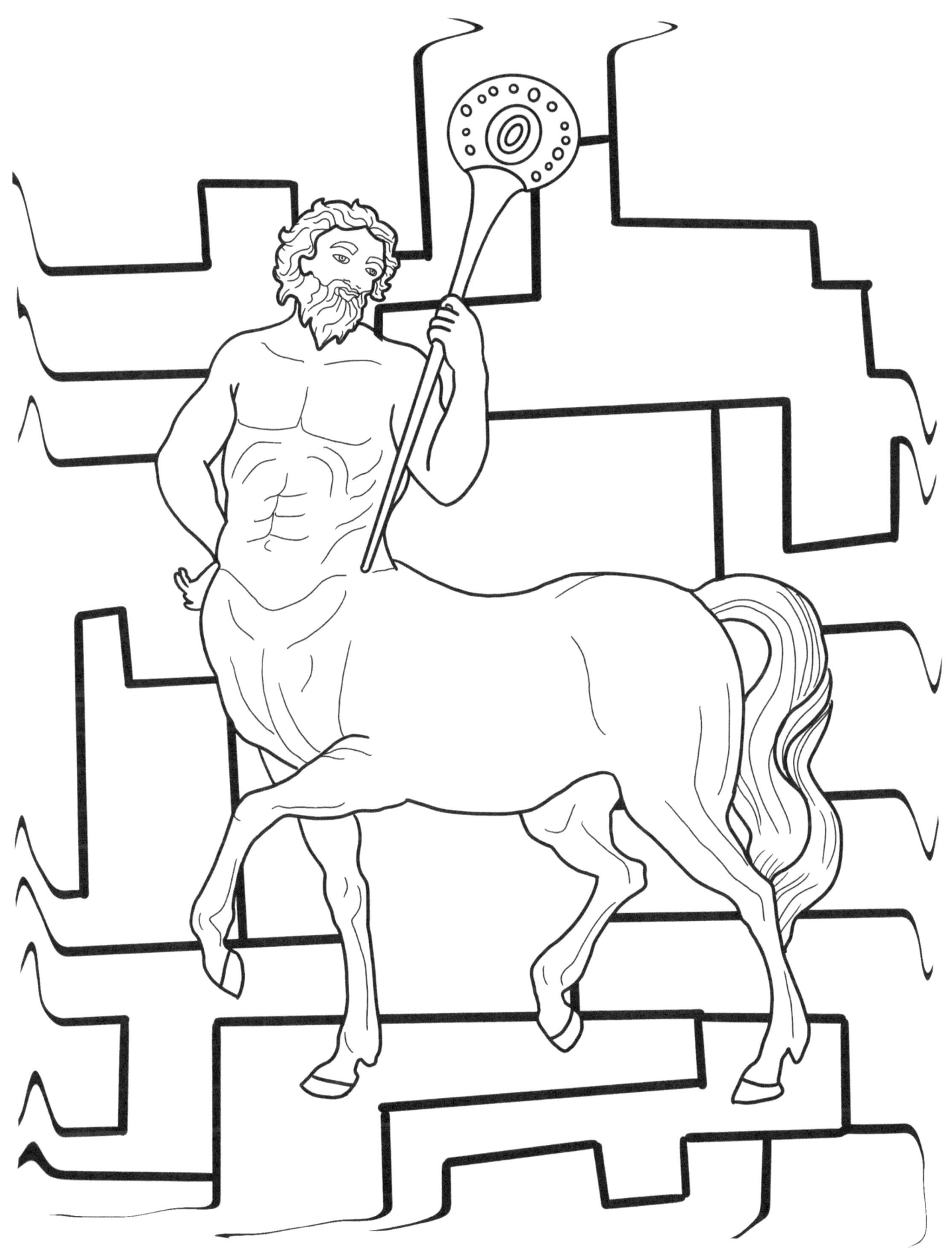

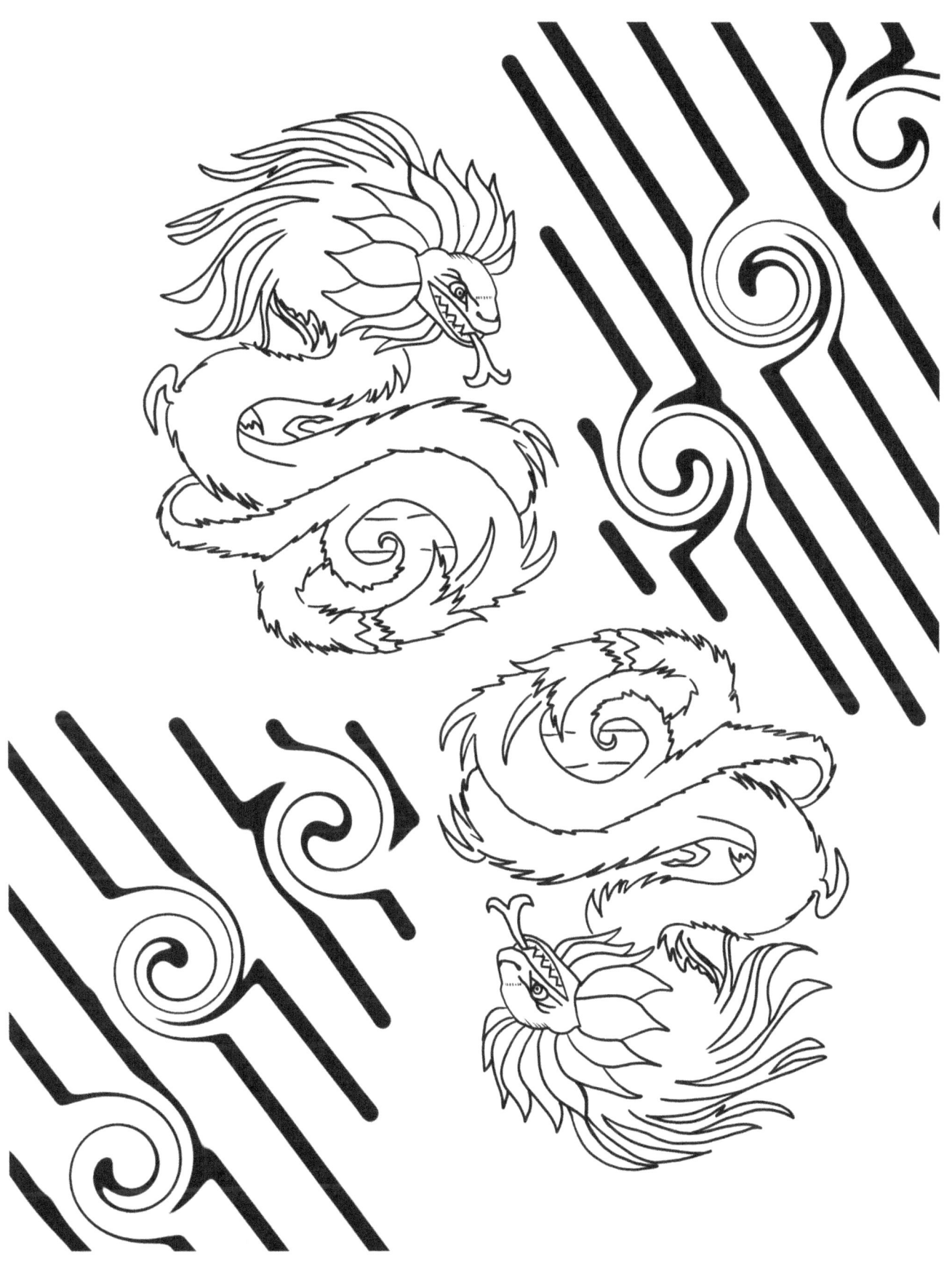

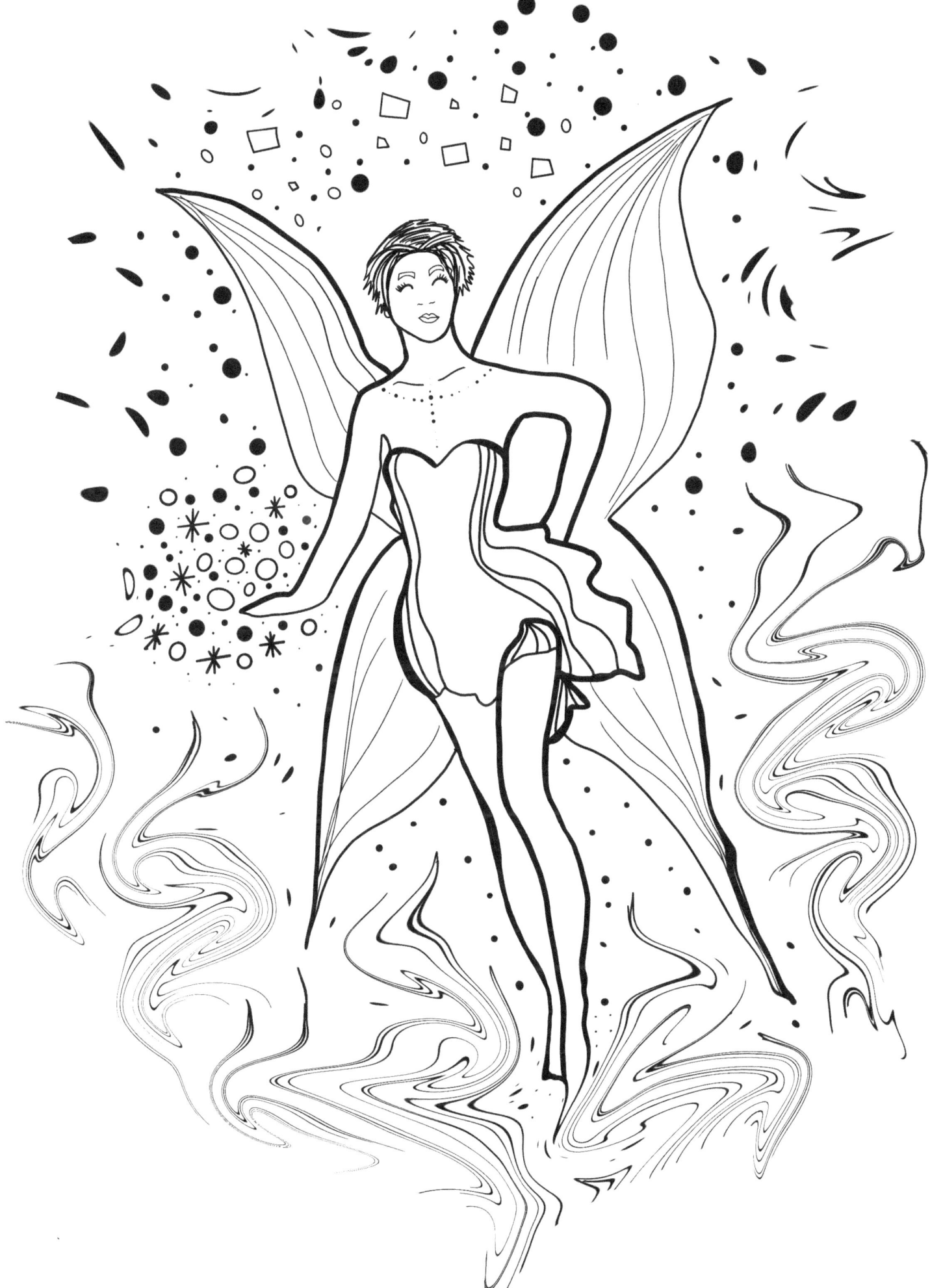

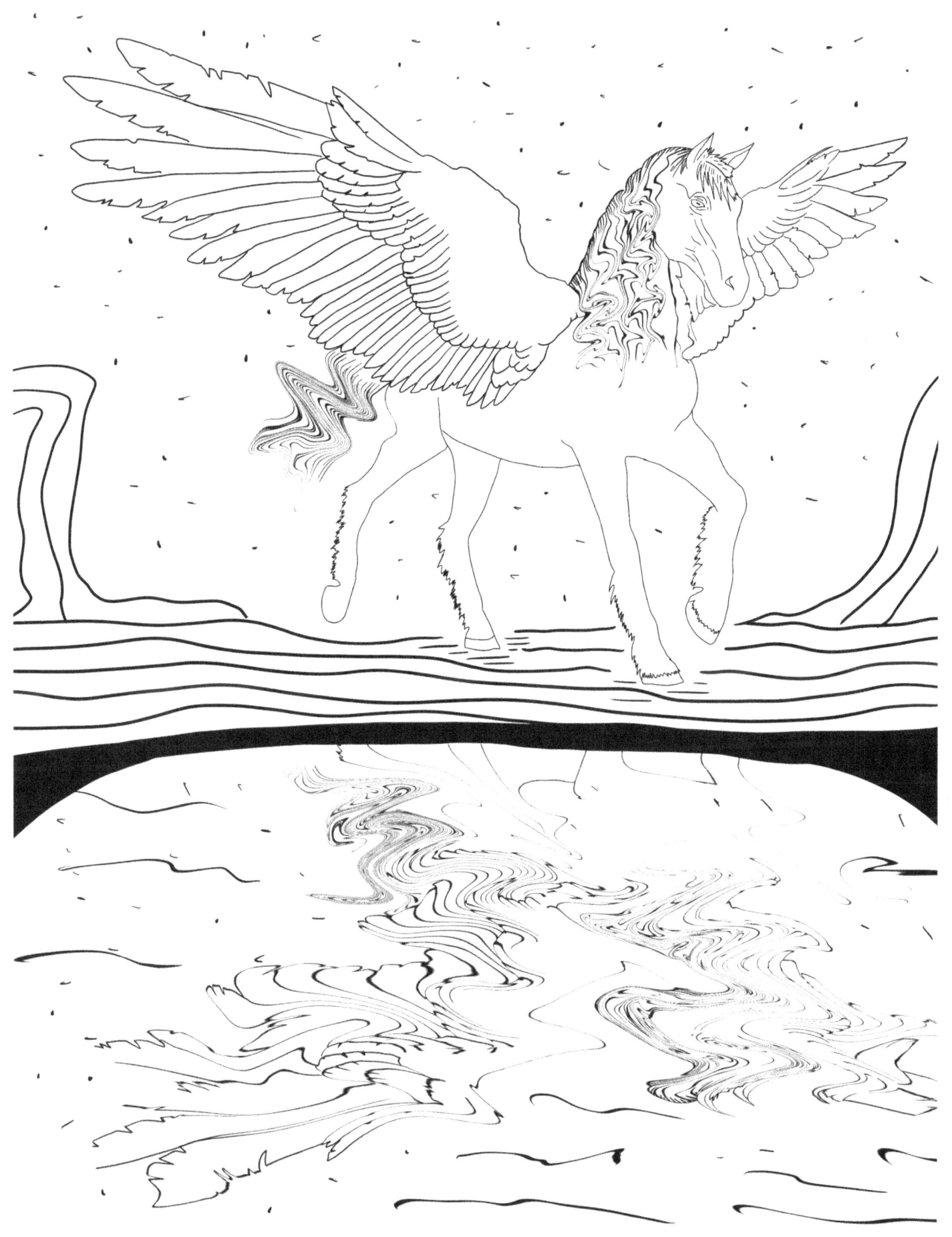

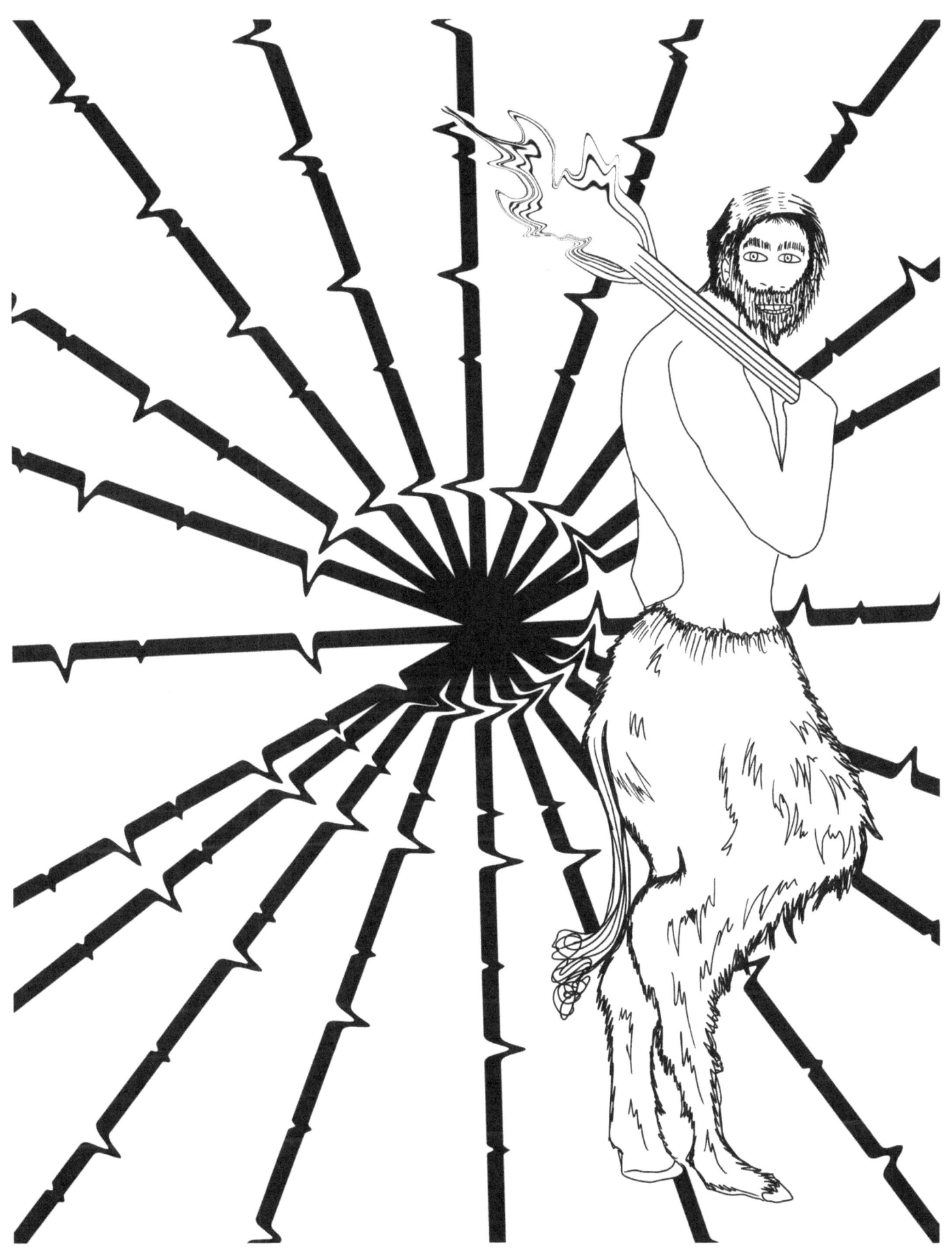

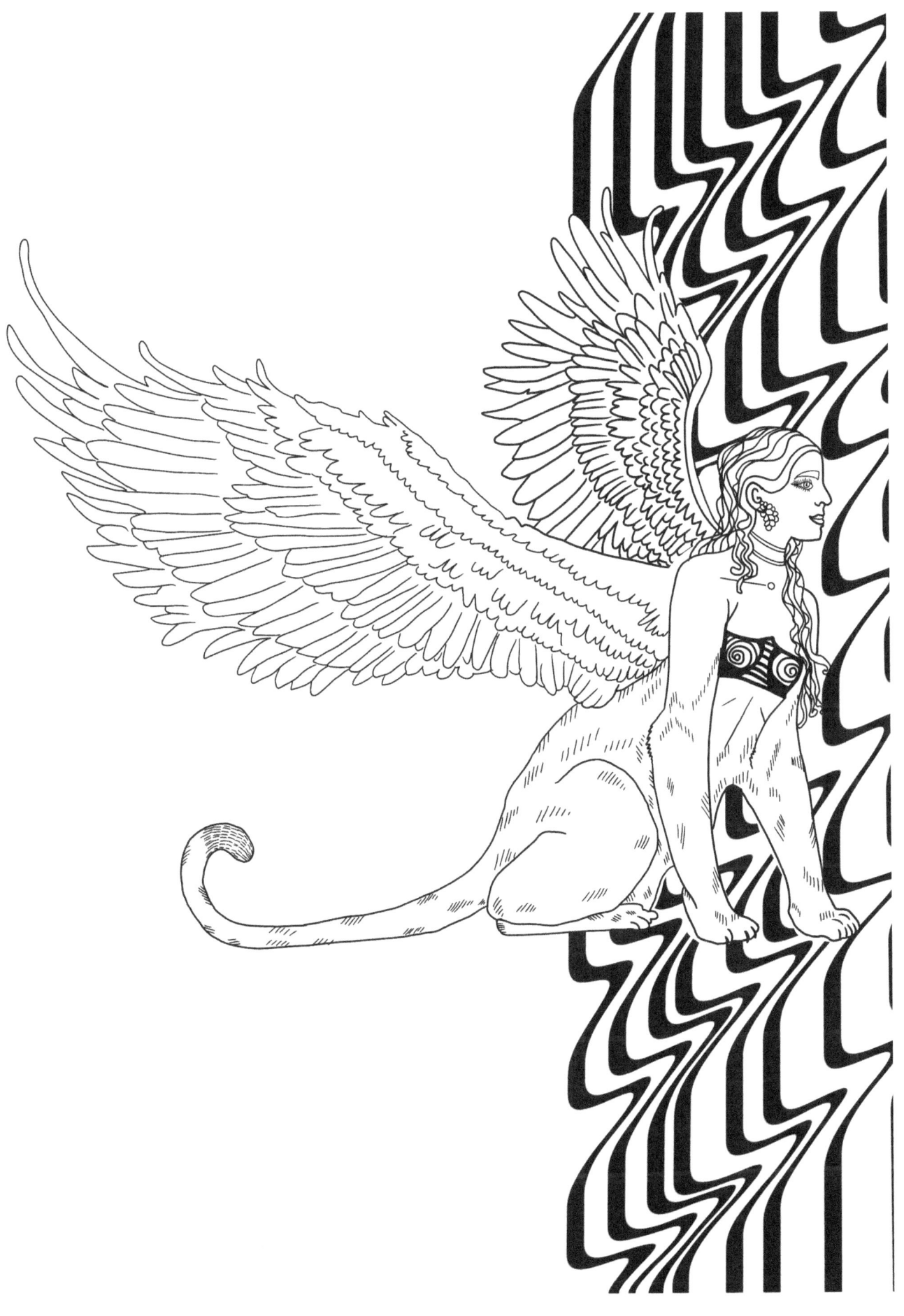

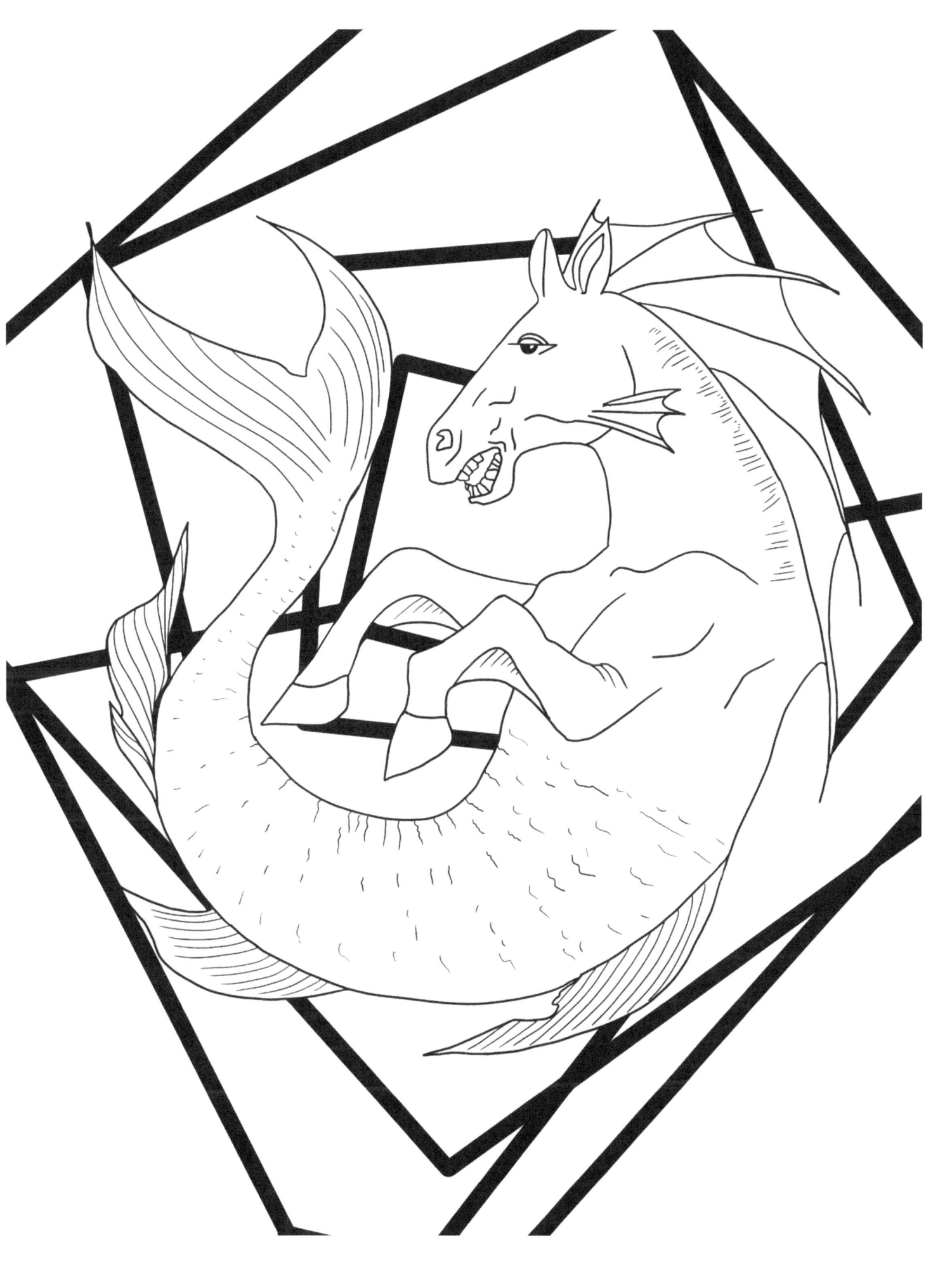

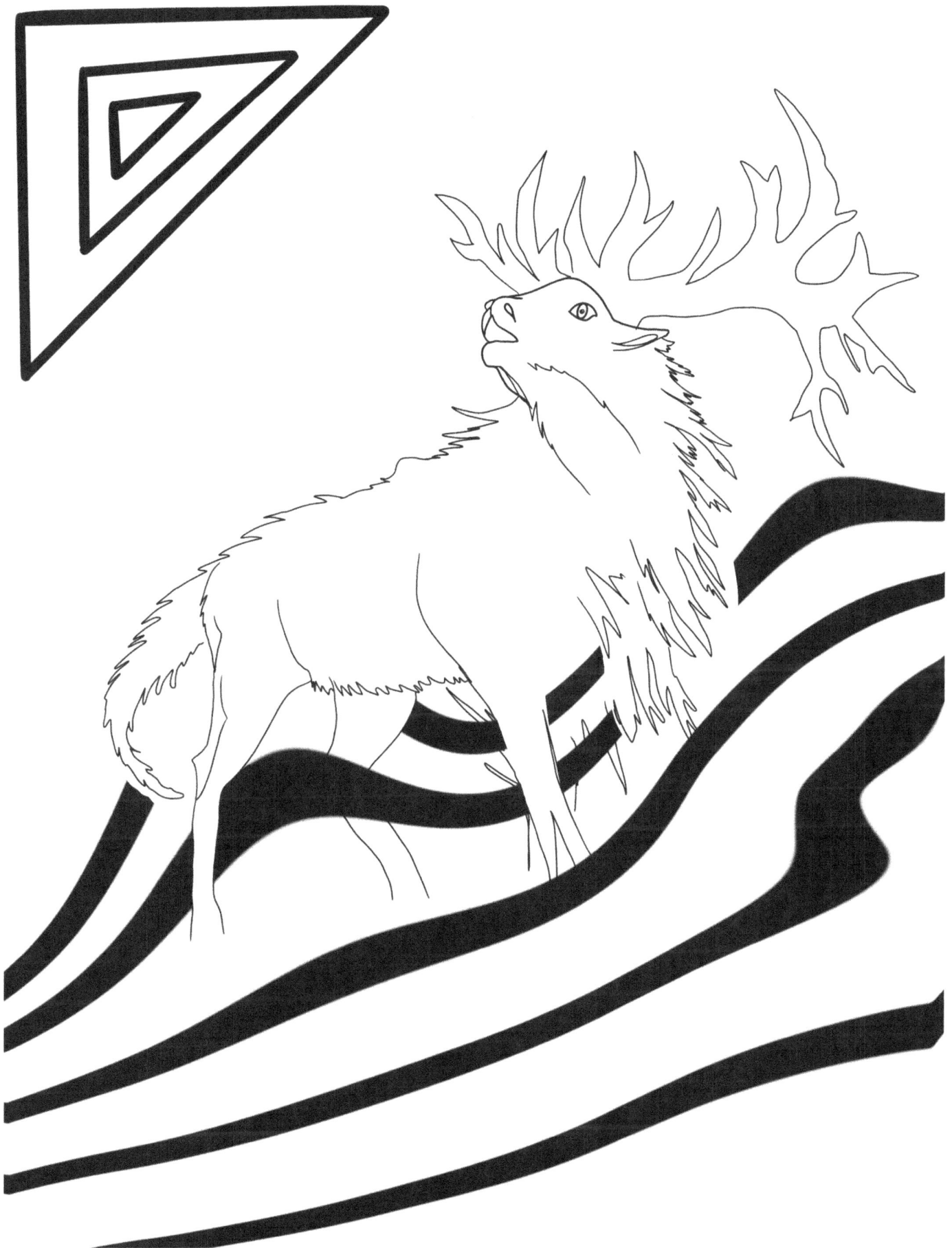

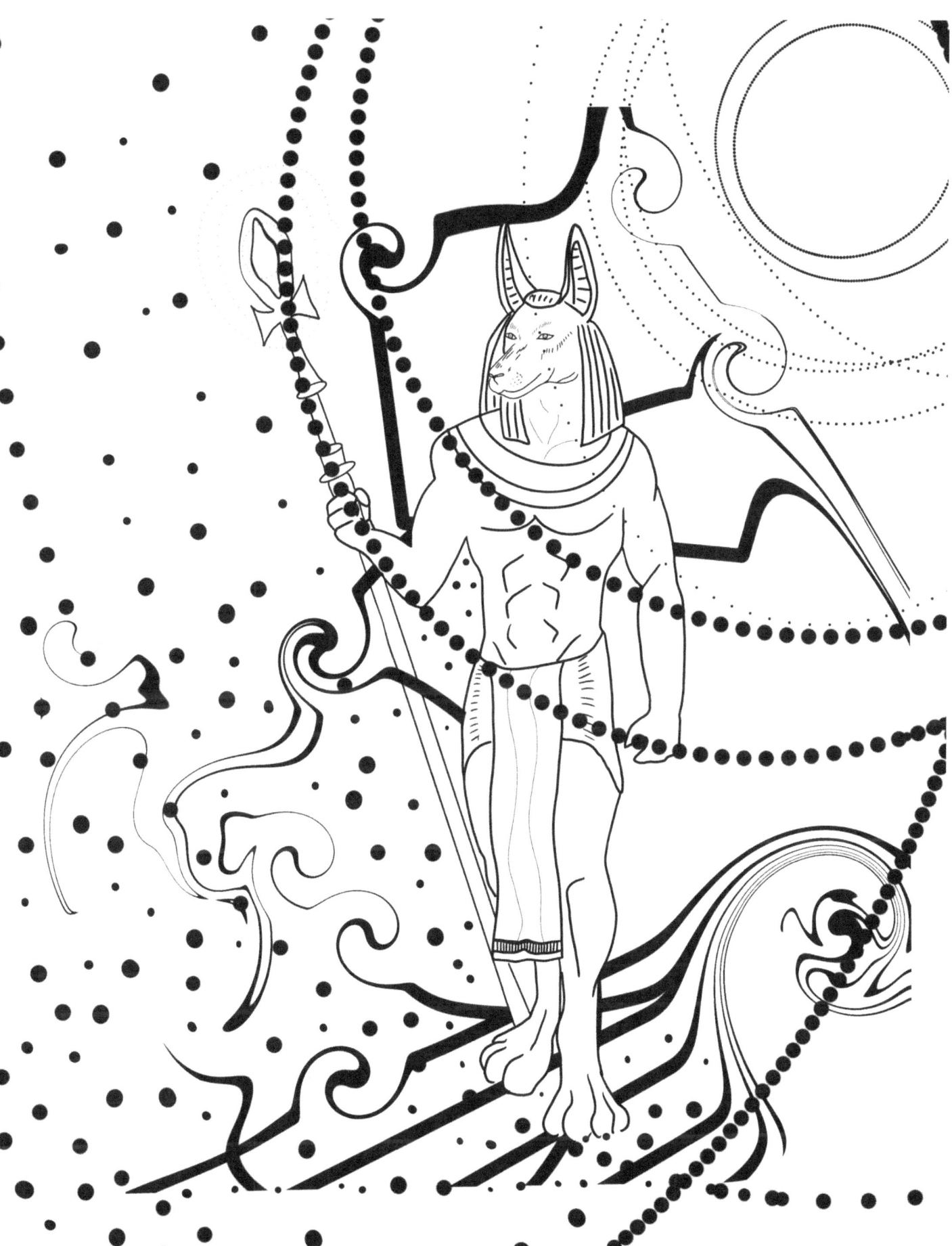

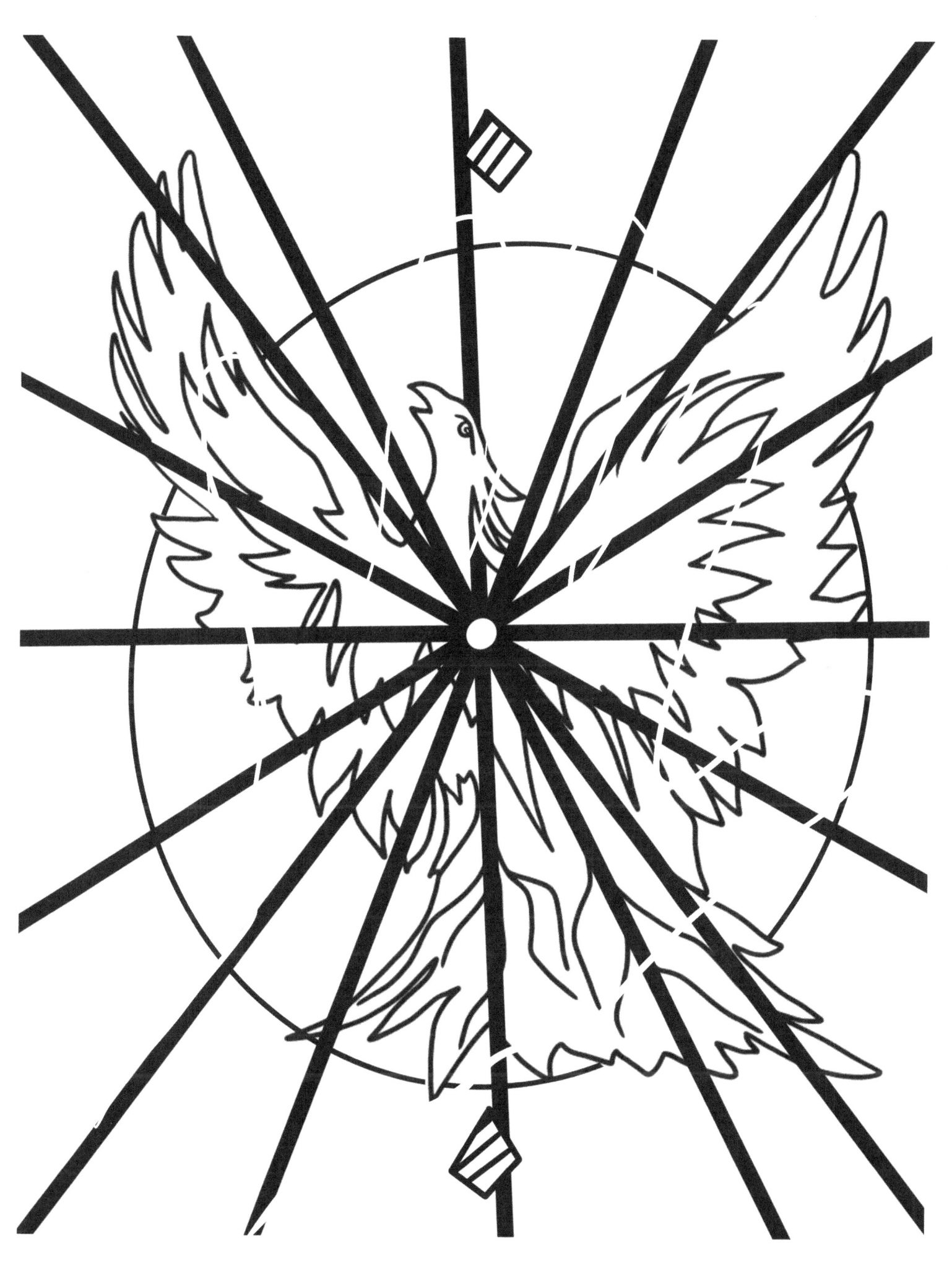

www.ingramcontent.com/pod-product-compliance
Lightning Source LLC
Chambersburg PA
CBHW081059240526
45465CB00025B/2762